THE
MATCHG[

Book and Lyrics
BILL OWEN

Music by
TONY RUSSELL

SAMUEL   FRENCH

LONDON

NEW YORK   TORONTO   SYDNEY   HOLLYWOOD

CHARACTERS

MATCHGIRLS	OTHERS
Kate	Annie Besant
Polly	George Bernard Shaw
Mrs Purkiss	Paula Westerby
Old Min	Scots Girl
Maggie	Foreman Mynel
Jessie	Mr Potter
Winnie	DOCKERS
Dot	Joe
Beattie	Perce
Nell	Bert
Louie	Tom

(These are the main characters, but any number of Matchgirls can be used)

(Paula Westerby and Scots Girl can be doubled. Mynel and Potter can double as Dockers. Any number of Dockers can be used. Shaw and two Dockers can be used as Directors in the "Waiting Song")

SYNOPSIS OF SCENES

ACT I

ACT II

SYNOPSIS OF MUSICAL NUMBERS

ACT I

SCENE 1	Phosphorus	The Matchgirls
	'Atful of 'ope	Mrs Purkiss and Girls
SCENE 2	Look Around	Kake and Matchgirls
	Me	Joe and Dockers
	Men	Kate, Polly, Joe, Perce
	La di dah	Beattie, Maggie, Polly, Jessie, Joe, Perce, two Dockers
SCENE 3	Something about you	Joe and Kate
SCENE 4	(reprise) Something about you	Bert and Winnie
	Mind you, Bert	The Matchgirls, Dockers
SCENE 5	Dear Lady	Kate, Annie
SCENE 6	We're gonna show 'em	Kate, Annie, Matchgirls
SCENE 7	(reprise) We're gonna show 'em	The Matchgirls, Annie, Kate

ACT II

SCENE 1	Cockney Sparrers	Polly, Matchgirls, Joe, Dockers
	Comes a time	Kate, Joe
SCENE 3	This life of mine	Kate, Company
SCENE 4	(reprise) Comes a time	Joe, Jessie
SCENE 5	Amendment to a motion	Old Min, Dockers, Girls
SCENE 6	Waiting	The Matchgirls, Dockers
SCENE 8	(reprise) This life of mine	The Company

AUTHOR'S NOTE

In this new edition of *The Matchgirls* I have made some alterations to both book and lyrics, my reasons being to simplify the staging and give the story more flow for amateur production.

Two songs have been deleted, "I long to see the day" and "The Hopping Dance", and a new number entitled "The La di dah" has been added which you will find inserted in the musical score. Several lyrics have been rewritten, and the songs "Life of mine" and "Comes a time" have been given a new setting in the play. Therefore, all reference to lyrics and musical continuity are to be found in this publication.

My advice to Producers in staging is "keep it simple", scenes can be made by "suggestion", using the minimum of impedimenta, maximum change of lighting and the use of sound effects wherever possible. The basic set can be curtains or flats of a neutral colour, with the exception of the Prompt and OP flats which might be painted as walls, the street lamp might be attached to either one. In Scene 1 the whole atmosphere of the monotony of cutting matches could be done in mime, the two benches can then be moved to the back of the set to form permanent rostrums and giving another acting level when required. "Hope Court" can be suggested by a line of washing quickly suspended high across the back of the set. "The Freethought Bookshop" needs only a table with a few pamphlets and papers, a chair and perhaps an old-fashioned hat stand. The scene "The Drawing Room at St John's Wood" is the only opportunity to show any kind of opulence in the entire play and I would suggest the use of beautiful and delicate furniture. A table, a couple of chairs with a rich-looking screen or hanging lace curtain as a background. Most of the remaining scenes can be performed on a bare stage. Try letting the Actors change the scenes as part of the action of the play. My best wishes for a successful show.

BILL OWEN

ACT I

SCENE 1

"The Corner" Cutting Room in the Match Factory, London. Spring, 1888

The early summer sunshine seeping through the one dirty window reveals a corner room where the work of cutting the matches is performed by the Girls. The work done here is much the same as on the main floor; the reason for its use is probably due to demand of the product. The only noise is that of monotonous work done by the Girls standing at benches

Maggie coughs a great deal, she suffers from TB. Polly, a lively girl, suddenly bursts into song, which comes to a stop as Mr Mynel, the foreman, appears round the corner. The Girls hurry with their work. When he leaves, Polly continues with her song; the Girls hush her. A Man, Mr Potter, walks through, carrying a large sack

Kate Mr Potter, 'ow's Rosy?

Several of the Girls "ssh" her

Garn, stuff 'im. 'Ow is she, Mr Potter?

More "sshing" from the Girls. Mr Potter puts a finger to his lips then takes a religious tract from his pocket and hands it to Kate

Mr Potter continues on his way and exits. At the same moment a "child of a girl" called Louie enters carrying a large empty tray on her head. She is a "carrier"

Louie collects the cut matches in the tray, puts the tray down by Jessie and pulls her shawl tight over her head. Kate meanwhile reads the pamphlet

'E's orf 'is nut!

Mrs Purkiss, a middle-aged woman, "ssshes" Kate. Louie picks up the tray of matches. She staggers as she attempts to put it on her head. The tray slips and several bundles of matches fall to the floor

Jessie You clumsy little cow!

More "sshing" from the Girls, Louie and Jessie start to pick up the bundles

Louie (*sotto voce*) I don't feel well.
Jessie (*sotto voce*) Well what d'yer come to work for then?

Mynel appears

Mynel The fine for droppin' matches is one penny.
Kate The kid can't 'elp it she ain't well.

Mynel (*to Kate*) And the fine for talkin' is one penny.

Mynel jots down in his book then looks around the room at the rest of the Girls

Anybody else got anything to say?

The Girls are silent. Mynel takes a whistle from his pocket and blows a shrill blast. The Girls stop work and begin to get their food

Mynel returns to his office

(*As he goes*) Quick enough when it's yer dinner ain't yer?

Maggie (*to Kate*) Did Mr Potter say 'ow Rosy was?

Kate No.

Mrs Purkiss I saw Mrs Potter yesterday, she said 'er teef 'ave all started to go loose.

Maggie Well, that's the beginnin' of the end.

Kate (*angrily*) It's always the same when you ask old Potter, 'e gives yer a pamphlet. (*She reads from the tract Potter gave her*) Listen to this. "Gawd is love . . . Gawd is the answer . . ." What does it mean?

Louie I wish Gawd'd find the answer to this. Look I got nuffin' between my bread.

Dot Ain't you lucky. (*Looking inside her sandwich*) Drippin' my old lady calls it—bleedin' cart grease.

Old Min I gotta pig's trotter.

Polly Pickled in gin, I bet.

Louie What you got, Beattie?

Beattie Same as you, bread and bread.

Winnie I got jam.

Jessie I'll change yer for a bit of cheese.

Polly I got a nice bit of bacon.

Maggie I just got marge.

Nell I got some chittlings.

Frances Some people 'ave all the luck.

Kate We got more than luck. (*She signals to the Girls*) There's one thing we've all got between our bread.

Girls And what's that?

The daily song of defiance is sung in the direction of Mynel's office. During it the Girls sit around on benches or stools to eat their food. Old Min sits alongside Winnie, a very pregnant girl who is the daughter of Mrs Purkiss

MUSIC: PHOSPHORUS

(*Singing*) Top grade selectable
'Ardly detectable
Phosphorus, phosphorus
Taste is more subtler and
Spreads just like butter grand
Phosphorus, phosphorus.

> Our special beauty cream
> We look a proper dream—for
> We are minus a jaw
>
> Guvnors don't charge a fee
> Give it away for free
> Phosphorus, phosphorus.

The music continues

Mynel appears from his office

Mynel Watch it, watch it.

Kate You can't fine us for singin' durin' feedin' time, Mr Mynel.

Mynel I got my eye on you.

Kate Which one?

The Girls roar with laughter

Mynel retires to his office in a temper

> Come on girls, let's 'ave a second chorus.

Girls We eat it every day
> Then it eats us away
> Phosphorus, phosphorus
> Posh folk eat caviare
> Oh, but we much prefer
> Phosphorus, phosphorus.

> Nice wooden overcoat
> Made of the finest oak
> Hooray getting buried today.
> Never respectable
> Always detectable
> Phosphorus, phosphorus.

Old Min Blimey, Win, you get any bigger you'll take orf.

Jessie I reckon she's gonna 'ave twins.

Winnie More likely a couple of 'omin' pigeons, that's all my Bert ever talks about.

Dot D'yer love 'im, Win?

Winnie (*surprised*) Do I what?

Dot D'yer love 'im?

Winnie (*almost undecided*) Well . . .

Mrs Purkiss 'Course she loves 'im. 'E put 'er in the fam'ly way, didn't 'e?

Louie looks down at her bare feet

Louie I wish I 'ad some boots.

Mrs Purkiss Ask Mrs Potter to give yer young Rosy's. She won't be needin' 'em no more.

Kate (*to Louie*) 'Ow much you get last week?

Louis Four 'n tuppence.

Kate 'Ow can anybody live on that?

Jessie She's only a carrier.

Polly I got nine bob; they stopped me tenpence in fines. I fink I'll 'ave to go to work on old Mynel.

Mynel enters from his office

Old Min I'd sooner pay the fines.

The Girls see Mynel and lapse into silence. He is about to exit when he notices Frances

Mynel Come 'ere, you.

Frances goes to him

What's that mark on your chin?

Frances is scared, she wipes her chin

Frances Nuffin', Mr Mynel—just dirt.

Mynel Let's 'ave a look, open yer mouf.

Frances does so

Wider. (*He looks into her mouth*)

Kate I suppose if she's got the phossy you'll sack 'er.

Mynel (*to Kate*) I'm warnin' yer. You fink because you're workin' round 'ere off the main floor I don't know what goes on. I can smell trouble-makers a mile orf.

Mynel exits

Polly gives Mynel the "razz"

Kate Frances, let's 'ave a look.

Kate looks into Frances's mouth

You ain't got no phossy in there.

Dot follows Mynel to the door and looks out

Old Min What's that red mark on 'er chin?

Nell That's 'ow it starts.

Frances I just scratched it.

Kate She's got no phossy in 'er norf and souf, I tell yer.

Dot All clear.

Mrs Purkiss Right, Totty Club. Nell, see if he's left his bowler on his desk.

Nell runs off

Polly, get the paper.

Polly goes to a box on her work bench

Jessie, get a pencil.

Jessie runs to her place on the bench

Louie (*very excitedly*) The Totty Club, The Totty Club—we're gonna draw the Totty Club.

Polly Louie, stop gettin' excited . . .

Louie dances around

Nell returns with a bowler hat. She hands the bowler to Mrs Purkiss

Winnie I wouldn't 'arf like to draw it this week. I'd buy a pair of sheets.

Old Min Swankpot.

Dot Just think, somebody's gonna put their 'and in that bowler in a minute and pick out that bit of paper . . .

Nell And it'll be the one—

Louie —the one wiv the cross on it.

Maggie I 'ope it's me.

Louie No, me . . . me . . . me . . .

Louie ⎱ The Totty Club, Totty Club, we're gonna draw the ⎰ (*Speaking*
Maggie ⎰ Totty Club.   ⎱ *together*)

Jessie returns with the pencil, and Polly with the paper

Mrs Purkiss Kate, tear that paper up and mark one bit wiv a cross.

Kate tears the paper into pieces, and prepares to mark one piece. Old Min tries to look over her shoulder

Min, keep your beady eyes orf. Right, let's 'ave yer twopences.

The Girls give their money to Mrs Purkiss. Old Min tries not to notice

Min!

Old Min reluctantly hands over her coppers. Kate folds the small slips of paper, they are emptied into the hat. Mrs Purkiss shakes the hat

MUSIC: 'ATFUL OF 'OPE

Mrs Purkiss	Look at that hat.
Girls	Just a dirty bowler hat.
Mrs Purkiss	There it is, now take a look at it.
Girls	Look at it, look at it.
	Look at that hat.
Mrs Purkiss	Butcher's 'ook at that hat
	That's no ordinary hat
	There's a titfer that's fit fer a
	Queen to be seen in
	That beautiful hat.
Girls	Close our eyes make a wish
	'Ave a dream while we may
	Cross yer fingers 'cause this
	Could be our lucky day.
Mrs Purkiss	Take a look at that hat
	Extraordinary hat.
	Someone ought to write a book on it

	Look on it, look on it. Look at that hat.
Maggie	If I wins it I'll get me 'at wiv an ostrich fevver And a brim that's oh so wide.
Nell	If I wins it I'll buy me a pair of button boots What does up at the side.
Jessie	I'll buy me a pretty petticoat Yus one wiv a scalloped 'em.
Beattie	I'll buy me a pair of fancy drawers.

The music stops

Mrs Purkiss	Now who the 'ell sees them?

The music starts

Polly	If I wins I'll buy myself a lovely silken blouse Wiv a fancy jewelled pin.
Old Min	If I wins I'll buy me a luv'ly barrel of bitter And a nice big bottle of gin.
Beattie	If I wins it I'll buy me a scarlet fancy shawl And knock the fellers dead.
Louie	If I wins it I'll buy me a second-hand royal tiara.
Mrs Purkiss	She's gorn right orf 'er 'ead.
Dot	I'll buy me a feather boa Just watch me when I'm out.
Louie	I'll buy me a summer bonnet
Old Min	And four dozen bottles of stout.
Kate	If I wins I'll buy my Joe A luv'ly painted box To keep 'is pigeons in
Winnie	If I wins I'll have me a great big luv'ly weddin'
Old Min	And annuver bottle of gin.

During the song, Mrs Purkiss takes the hat around for the Girls to draw their slip of paper. So far, no-one has been successful. Then it is Old Min's turn, she dips her hand into the hat and, all of a shake, she unfolds the slip of paper. Then she screams

I got it . . . I got it!!

The Girls sing and dance another chorus of "'Atful of 'ope"

Girls (*singing*) She's got it!

	With her bottle of stout
	They won't know her when she's out
	Lookin' just like a queen
Old Min	Wiv me bottle of gin
Mrs Purkiss	Wiv'er bottle of gin
Girls	Though there don't seem much 'ope
	We just manage to cope and that's that
	Till we look, till we look
	Take a look
	Take a look at that hat.

A Girl rushes on

Girl 'Ere, 'ave you 'eard, they're gonna stop a shillin' for Gladstone's statue.

There is uproar from the Girls

Kate They ain't got no right to stop money out of our wages.
Mrs Purkiss Not wivout our permission . . .
Polly Up Gladstone, that's what I say.
Old Min And 'is little black bag.
Dot Let 'em pay for their own bloody statue.
Kate We took enough I tell yer, they fine us fer talkin', fer droppin' matches, fer 'avin' dirty feet.
Old Min They'll fine us for breathin' next.
Polly Don't give 'em ideas.
Kate I say they ain't got no right to stop money out of our wages for a statue—

The Girls yell agreement

—wivout askin' us first.
Jessie But they're goin' to, ain't they?
Kate But I say they ain't got not right.

There is an outburst from the Girls. Kate attempts to quieten them. They continue to argue and shout as the scene changes

SCENE 2

Hope Court. That evening

A dingy court, surrounded by slum tenements. Kate is still attempting to get quiet. During the following scene, Mr Potter walks across trying to distribute tracts. Most of the Girls—knowing him—ignore it. Standing in the shadows is Annie Besant

Kate All right—quiet a minute—quiet. Now, listen all of yer!
Mrs Purkiss Shut yer gobs all of yer . . . You've been yellin' since lunch time—but not when Old Mynel was about! So listen to Kate!

The Girls quieten down

Kate Does any of yer want this statue of Gladstone?
Polly Not me. Couldn't get it in our front room.
Old Min I never knew Gladstone was alive till I 'eard 'e was dead.
Dot 'E ain't dead—'e's the Prime Minister.
Old Min Everbody's got an excuse.
Kate Do we want this statue?
Girls No!
Kate I say if they want it—let them pay for it.

The Girls yell in agreement

Jessie But they're gonna stop the shilling from our wages . . . so what can
we do?
Kate But they ain't allowed to do it—it's against the law.
Nell (*sarcastically*) What do you know about the law?
Mrs Purkiss They don't make laws for the likes of us.
Maggie But Kate's right, we've got to stop 'em.
Jessie 'Ow we gonna stop 'em? Come on, Miss Know-All, tell me 'ow?
Old Min Nobody can stop 'em, nobody can beat 'em—you'll learn.
Kate But there must be a way—there must be!

*Annie Besant emerges from the shadows. She is a handsome, well-dressed
woman in her thirties*

Annie There is a way to beat them!

The Girls turn and view her with suspicion

There is a way to stop them!

Polly and Jessie walk around her

Polly (*in a posh voice*) Hi say, it must be Lady Muck.
Jessie Jolly naice day, old bean—what!
Polly Yers—it's the wevver you know.

The Girls laugh

Kate What do you want?
Annie May I talk with you?
Mrs Purkiss What can the likes of you 'ave to say to us?
Annie You work in that match factory?
Winnie Oh no, we just go there for our summer 'olidays.
Kate Why should that concern you?
Annie My name is Annie Besant. I'm writing an article for a weekly
journal.
Dot You mean a newspaper?
Maggie D'yer want my life story?
Beattie You could write it down on a postage stamp
Annie It's called *The Link*.
Mrs Purkiss Never 'eard of it

Annie It's published by the Fabian Society.
Polly I 'ope it keeps fine for yer.
Kate You mean you want to write about us in your paper?
Annie And your working conditions.
Mrs Purkiss Watch it, Kate. If the guvnors was to 'ear about this . . .
Kate 'Ow do we know who you are? Comin' down 'ere nosin' around.
You want to know what it's like to work in there why don't yer try it
yerself?
Annie If necessary I'll do that!

The two "firebrands" face each other

One of our members is a factory inspector, she was down here a week
ago.
Kate We 'ave all the "do gooders" down 'ere. I expect it eases their
conscience.
Mrs Purkiss What conscience?
Annie We're on your side.
Nell Nobody's on our side except us.
Annie Well I'm on your side—whether you like it or not!!
Kate (*after a pause*) What d'yer want to know?
Annie What it's like to work in there. I want you to tell me—in your own
words.
Beattie Words!
Jessie What words!
Kate 'Ow can the likes of me find the words to tell you the 'ell we 'as to live
through in there?
Annie Try.

MUSIC: LOOK AROUND

Kate (*speaking*) 'Ave you ever seen a girl
                    What's old before she's young—
     (*singing*) 'Ave you ever seen two eyes
                    So tired they couldn't cry a tear?
                    'Ave you ever seen a 'ead so bowed
                    It never sees the sky?
                    Look around, dear lady, look around.
Maggie Tell 'er about the phossy jaw, Kate.
Dot And what it does to yer.
Girls (*singing*) 'Ave you ever seen a girl
                    What's old before she's young?
                    'Ave you ever seen a face
                    That looks like winter all the year?
                    'Ave you ever gone to sleep
                    And never cared if you should wake?
                    Look around, dear lady—look around.

Winnie Tell 'er about the wages, Kate.
Jessie And the place where we 'as to earn 'em.
Annie I want to help you—you must trust me.
Kate (*singing*)   'Ave you ever seen a girl
                What's old before she's young?
                Have you ever heard her laughter
                Sound like crying to the wind?
                If you want to see how living
                Is just waiting till you die,
All   Look around, dear lady, look around.
Kate   Look around dear lady, look around.

As the song finishes, the Girls stand facing Annie

Annie I do want to help you—you must trust me.
Mrs Purkiss Why should we trust you any more than the others?

Before Annie can go on, Joe and his mates enter. They are dockers

The mood of the scene changes. There is "skylarking" between the Girls and the Fellers

Joe What yer, Kate.

Kate rushes to Joe; they kiss passionately. Annie seems a little surprised at this complete lack of inhibition

        'Evenin', Mrs Besant.
Annie (*surprised*) Good evening, I . . .
Kate 'Ere, 'ow do yer know Mrs Besant?
A Docker Most of the dockers know Mrs Besant.
A Docker Some of 'em wouldn't mind knowin' 'er a bit better.

The Men roar with laughter

Joe We 'ear you spoutin' every mornin' outside the dock gates. Mind you, we don't 'ave much time to listen. You see, we 'as to work.
Annie You're one of the lucky ones.
A Docker (*cynically*) Oh yus, we're lucky—look at us.
Joe That's our middle name.
Kate (*breaking in*) Mrs Besant's goin' to 'elp us, Joe.
Joe Anybody wants to 'elp me down 'ere I get suspicious.
Annie Why should you be suspicious of me?
Joe Why? Where d'you live, Mrs Besant?
Annie St John's Wood.
Joe Different up there, ain't it? Two 'ansoms up the drive. Plenty of servants around to dust all yer books on socialism.
Kate Mrs Besant want to know what we 'as to go thru'. 'Ow we 'ave to live. She wants to 'elp us.

MUSIC: ME

Joe There's only one way to know
What it's like to live down here.
Dockers That's to live down 'ere!
Joe There's only way way to know
How you can survive down here.
Dockers Stay alive down here!
Kate (*angrily*) But that's all we're doin', just stayin' alive.
Annie What about the thousands of dockers that wait like animals outside those dock gates every morning? For what? The pittance of a few hours work at fourpence halfpenny an hour.
Joe That's right. We are animals. They treat us like animals. They put us in a cage—did you know that? Then the foreman walks around like 'e's at a cattle market.

Joe does a little play-acting with the Dockers as he walks around prodding, pinching and "goosing"

Yes, you—and you.
A Docker (*imitating a "whining man"*) Me, sir—don't forget me—me—me.
Joe (*swinging back to Annie*) And me—the foreman never passes me by. There's always a ticket for Joey boy.
Annie And that's all you care.

MUSIC: ME

Joe Care!
Would they care about me?
Dockers There's only one way to know
What it's like to live down here,
That's to live down here!
There's only one way to know
How you can survive down here
Stay alive down here!
Joe As I go my way
The one thing I care about
The thing I'm gonna beware about
Is me, me, me, me, me . . .
Wherever I go,
There ain't no son of a gun
Can put it over on Number One,
Not me, me, me, me, me . . .
When a bloke calls me brother,
Says "how yer doing Joe"—
I reach for my pocket
To see that I've still got my dough.
As I go my way,
I don't have no doubt of it,

What am I gonna get out of it—
Is the only kinda motto what'll pay;
For me, me, me, me, me . . .

At the end of the chorus, Kate rushes at Joe. The music continues

Kate 'Oo do you fink you are?
Joe Me, me, me, me, me.

The Dockers roar with laughter

Dockers Me, me, me, me, me.
Annie I'll write this article, Kate. It'll be a start. Will you help me?
Kate 'Course we will. I'll walk down the road wiv yer. (*She looks at Joe*)
You can't trust the men around 'ere.

Annie and Kate exit

The others go into a "ME" routine

  At the end of the dance, some of the Girls and Boys wander off

The remaining Boys and Girls stand around, talking

  Kate comes storming back

Where was you dragged up, Joe Burton?
Joe In the same street as you, remember?
Kate Why did you 'ave to be so rude to Mrs Besant?
Joe I wasn't rude, I was just puttin' my point of view.
Kate 'Oo asked yer for it?
Joe Nobody. But then nobody ever asks 'er for 'ers. But, mate, when Mrs
Besant's 'andin' out advice, it's every man for 'imself.
Kate Well, we trust 'er—she's gonna 'elp us.
Joe And the best of luck. To me she's just another "do gooder".
Kate She's different, I tell yer.
Joe You can say that again. What time I see yer tonight?
Kate (*sulking*) I dunno.
Joe Please yerself.

  Joe moves off

Bert Anyone coming down the Anchor for a pint?

  *The Men and Girls, except Kate, walk off. At that moment, Polly enters,
  followed by Perce, her feller*

Polly Lay off me.
Kate (*calling off*) Joe!
Perce What was you doin' out with Ginger Carter last night?
Kate (*calling off*) I'll see yer tonight, Joe!
Polly Not the same as when I'm out wiv you; 'e 'appens to be a gentle-
man.
Perce You're supposed to be my donah.
Kate (*calling off*) JOE!

Polly (*angrily*) I'm nobody's donah. Just 'cause you buy a girl a small port you wanna put a ticket on 'er back "Reserved".

Perce (*becoming tough*) Listen . . .

Polly (*becoming tougher*) No you listen! I belong to nobody—and that's the way I like it.

Kate (*calling off, angrily*) All right then—go on yer own!

Polly (*referring to Kate*) Then I don't get blood pressure like 'er. Now go on—push yer barrer—go on—on yer way.

Perce (*disgustedly*) Women! Give me pigeons any time.

Perce exits

Kate and Polly stand looking after their men

MUSIC: MEN

Kate	What is it about that man?
	I'll never understand:
	He's either blowin' off his top
	Or eating out my hand—
	Love for me is never quiet
Polly	Love for me is one long riot
Both	Where are the wine and the roses?
	What the 'ell do you suppose is wrong
	With our love song?
	Men
	We always have trouble with men,
	They just drive yer right round the bend
Polly	They'll love yer and leave yer,
	They'll lie and deceive yer, will men
Both	Men
	On men you can never depend
Kate	I tell him we're through it's the end
	He's all brokenhearted—
	(And) I'm back where I started again
Polly	If I could find some place
	Where there was no man in sight,
	That's where I'd spend my days
Kate	You might spend your days,
	But never your nights
Polly (*speaking*)	Imagine a world without men.
Kate (*speaking*)	Don't torture yerself.
Polly	Men
	Now I'm a good starter with men—
	I know what they're after, my friend
Kate	If I could ignore him
	Instead I adore him, but then
Both	Men
	The species we can't comprehend
	The story-book romancers when

                        The mood kinda takes 'em
                        Oh why can't we hate 'em, these men

Joe and Perce enter

Polly   What do we see in them
                        I don't understand at all

The Men make up to the Girls

Men   But then a her meets him
                        And before you know it
                        She's starting to fall
                        Men
                        There's something about us we men
                        You can't do without us we men
                        It's just evolution
                        There's no substitution for men

The two couples dance

Joe Ta, ta you funny females.
Perce Keep yer 'and on yer 'alfpenny.

Joe and Perce exit

The two Girls are furious at being left, just as they were feeling "the urge"

Both (*singing*)   Men
                        Gone back to their pigeons again—
Polly   I feel like an old broody hen
Kate   You get that old feeling
                        And you hit the ceiling, but then
Polly   Men
                        They're always a trouble, these men—
                        Right since the damn world began
Kate   But if that fellow Adam
                        Had been born a madam—what then?
Both   AMEN!

Kate and Polly begin to exit

   Mr Potter enters carrying a banner which reads: "ARE YOU TIRED OF SIN?"

Kate 'Ello, Mr Potter.
Polly (*reading the poster*) What's this—"Are you tired of sin". Not yet, Mr Potter, but I'll let yer know.
Potter I am the light and the way.
Kate 'Ow's your Rosy?
Potter Suffer the little children to come unto me.
Polly All right, then—but 'ow's Rosy?
Potter The Lord giveth, the Lord taketh away.
Kate (*losing her temper*) Is that all you can do, spout the Bible?

Polly Lay orf him Kate—'e's orf 'is crumpet.

Louie enters, skipping with a rope

Kate But he never answers yer questions!
Louie Mr Potter, if your Rosy don't get better can I 'ave 'er boots?
Potter If the Lord calls I will bring her to Him.
Louie Can I 'ave 'er boots then?

Potter exits, chanting

Potter (*as he goes*) In my arms I will bring her to Him.
Louie (*calling after him*) Can I have her boots then Mr Potter? (*To Kate*) If I had some boots I could go to the unveilin'.
Kate You stay away from the unveilin'.
Louie The others are goin'.
Polly Well, 'ere's one that ain't!
Kate Nobody from our section will be there, you can rely on that.
Louie But we're supposed to go.

Perce enters. He wears a fancy waistcoat, a bright neckerchief and a "cocky" bowler worn at a rakish angle

Polly What are you all dolled up for?
Perce We're goin' on the La di dah.
Polly When?
Perce Tonight, of course. Up West. Yer comin'?
Polly (*playing hard to get*) Er I dunno—I'll 'ave to fink about it.
Perce What's there to fink about. You're either comin' or you ain't.
Polly I might 'ave other things to do.
Perce Like what?
Polly I've told yer, I'll think about it.
Perce Please yerself. (*He makes to move off*)
Polly (*suddenly*) I've thought about it!

Polly runs to Perce and they begin to move off, arms around each other. Perce turns to Kate

Perce Joe's expectin' you to come, Kate.
Kate Then why couldn't he ask me 'imself?
Perce 'E's feedin' his pigeons, ain't he.

Perce and Polly exit

Kate (*disgustedly*) Pigeons! (*She smiles*) But we'll be goin' on the La di dah. (*She starts to exit*)

Mrs Purkiss and Winnie enter

Mrs Purkiss Kate, 'ave you 'eard the latest?
Kate What?
Mrs Purkiss They ain't goin' to pay us for the couple of hours to go to this unveilin'.

Winnie They just posted a notice on the gates. Factory's closed till the afternoon.

Kate But they can't do that.

Winnie Then go and look at the notice on the factory gates if you don't believe me.

Kate begins pacing up and down in anger and frustration

Mrs Purkiss I reckon the word got about that our section wasn't goin', and some of the others was gonna do the same.

Kate They're not goin' to get away with this!

Winnie I'm goin' to 'ave a long lovely lie in bed.

Kate They're not I tell yer!

Mrs Purkiss Stop gettin' yerself all worked up Kate.

Winnie There's nuffin' we can do about it.

Kate There is, there must be!

Winnie If we ain't workin' they don' 'ave to pay us.

Mrs Purkiss I'll work—I'm willin' to work . . .

Kate Wait! I've got it. We're goin' to that unveilin'.

Winnie Not me!

Mrs Purkiss Are you orf your nut?

Kate We'll give 'em a surprise. Now we've got to find the others.

Mrs Purkiss What do yer mean, a surprise?

Kate Come on, let's find the others. I'll tell yer on the way.

Kate, Mrs Purkiss and Winnie exit

MUSIC: LA DI DAH

Beattie enters with a Docker, then Maggie likewise followed by Polly and Perce. The Girls are dressed in bright skirts and blouses, large fancy hats with feather boas draped around their shoulders. The Dockers are dressed like Perce. They dance jauntily to the musical intro. Then Joe enters dressed as the other Dockers

Joe (*looking around*) Where's Kate?

Louie She went off wiv Mrs Purkiss and Winnie, somethin' about the unveilin'.

Joe Didn't she leave a message?

Louie No, she just rushed orf.

Louie runs off as Jessie enters in her finery

Joe holds out his arm, she takes it and the "La di dah" begins

All (*singing*) When we're on the La di dah
                    We walk with a La di dah
                    That gives us an independent air
Girls   All full of airs and graces
                    With paint and powdered faces—
                    Why we hold up the traffic
                    All the way down Mile End Road

All	But then when we're on the La di dah
	We ain't what they think we are—
	We could be the aristocracy
Girls	Why, city gents will turn and stare
	When we step off the tram
Dockers	What they don't know, of course, is
	They're mutton dressed up as lamb
All	But we don't need a reason or a rhyme
	When it's La di dah, La di dah time.

Dockers	When we're on the La di dah
	We all share a posh cigar
	Which might last us up to Leicester Square
Girls	Of course, we keep on stopping
	To do our window shopping
Dockers	While we just stand around
	And try and look like millionaires
All	Of course, when we're on the La di dah
	We can go a bit too far—
	We gatecrashed a party in Mayfair
Girls	Champagne and oysters, caviare
	And waltzing round and round
Dockers	But we livened up the evening
	Doing "Knees up, Muvver Brown"
Girls	They was so drunk they didn't seem to mind
All	On that La di dah, La di dah time

They dance

	Because when we're on the La di dah
	We ain't who *we* think we are
	But dreaming costs nothing, though they say
Girls	That dreams won't make a lady
Dockers	But it's clothes what makes a man
All	But we don't need no excuses—
	So you'd better bring out the band
	For we don't need a reason or a rhyme
	When it's La di dah, La di dah
	Ring dem bells, sound the alarm
	La di dah
	La di dah
	T I M E ! !

SCENE 3

Down by the River Lea. Evening

This is the "oasis" for those in love to escape to. Joe is calling in his pigeons by tempting them with corn. Kate is seated on the scrubby grass leaning against the pigeon box as she excitedly recounts the unveiling. She has a bandage on her arm

Kate (*laughing*) You should 'ave seen 'em, Joe. All dressed up to the nines. There was all our guvnors, the Mayor and 'alf the Town 'All—wiv their wives. Talk about toffee nose—you should have seen their hats. They looked like Covent Garden, all fruit and flowers. Anyway after all the speeches the Mayor goes over to the statue and pulls a bit of string and down falls the Union Jack—and there was old Gladstone in marble. He looked quite sad. Now we've all been standing there as though butter wouldn't melt in our mouths ain't we—but when I gives 'em the signal—did we let 'em 'ave it! Rotten eggs, termaters, dustbin leavins—anything we could lay our 'ands on. The women started screamin'—coppers was blowin' their whistles . . .

She roars with laughter. Joe appears to be paying no attention

You listenin' Joe? (*After a pause*) Joe?
Joe What?
Kate You ain't heard a word I said.
Joe Yes I 'ave.
Kate Well?
Joe (*turning to her*) What good did it do yer?
Kate 'Ell of a lot. We 'ad a good laugh—and that's something we ain't 'ad for a long time.
Joe They're bound to 'ave got your number as the ringleader for a start.
Kate Old Mynel's always warnin' me. (*After a pause*) Stuff him. I don't care.
Joe And neither will any of these so called mates of yours when you get the sack.
Kate I'm not goin' to row wiv you tonight—it's no use tryin'. I ain't got the strength.
Joe (*referring to the bandage*) What you done to yer arm?
Kate I just cut it, it's nuffin'. Come and sit down. Your pigeons'll come back. That's more than I'd do if I was one of 'em.
Joe I know 'ow to get you back.
Kate I'd fly and I'd fly.
Joe 'T'ain't much fun bein' a pigeon, yer know.
Kate If you was a pigeon as well we wouldn't notice the difference would we? (*She pulls Joe down to her and kisses him passionately*) I love yer, Joe—I do love yer.
Joe (*extricating himself*) Yus—well—let me get the pigeons in first.
Kate (*furiously*) I wonder you don't make love to them!

She turns her back on him, Joe tries to get his pigeons in

Joe (*frantically*) Coop—coo—come on—come on in—d'yer wanna ruin me love life . . .?

Kate turns back and looks at him and smiles

MUSIC: *SOMETHING ABOUT YOU*

Kate There's something about you
Something different about you
Like no other Joe I know—
Not your looks or your walk,
Or the way that you talk,
Not a thing that I see
Makes yer special for me
But there's something about you
Makes me can't do without you—
And maybe I never will know
How to ever explain
Be it sunshine or rain
That with my arms about you,
There's something about you,
My love.

Joe There's something about you
Something different about you
Like no other girl I know—
Not your nose or your hair,
Or the clothes that you wear,
Not a thing that I see
Makes you special for me
But there's something about you
Makes me can't do without you—
And I know wherever I go
Not the time or the place,
Or the smile on your face
But with my arms about you—
Both There's something about you—my love.

SCENE 4

Hope Court. The Wedding

The music continues from the previous scene as a Light picks out Winnie as the bride, and Bert doing his best to look cheerful as the groom

MUSIC: *SOMETHING ABOUT YOU* (reprise)

Bert There's something about you
It's all round about you
Winnie You don't 'ave to tell me I know
Bert Bride and groom, you and me
Winnie And the baby makes three—
Bert But the weddin' was fine
Winnie Just in time, just in time—

Bert	But there's somethin' about you
	When I walk around you
Winnie	And you've got a long way to go
Bert	Just me pigeons and us
Winnie	I feel just like a bus
Both	But with my arms about you
	There's something about you, my love.

The Lights come on to reveal the Court hung with bunting, and all the guests enjoying the excuse for a "booze up". Jessie is making up to Joe in Kate's absence. Mrs Purkiss is the ever tearful, rather beerful mother-in-law as she goes to Bert

Mrs Purkiss You'll take good care of 'er won't yer Bert?

Bert (*bored*) I'll do me best, Mrs Purkiss.

Mrs Purkiss You must call me Mum now. (*As an order*) Well, go on, call me Mum!

Bert Yes, Mum.

Mrs Purkiss Take good care of 'er, she's me last. (*In tears*) They've all gorn and left their poor old Mum now.

Bert 'Ave they, Mum?

Mrs Purkiss Yus, Mum, they 'ave. You won't forget yer old Mum, will yer, you'll come and visit me now and then?

Winnie (*impatiently*) Oh blimey, Mum, we're only movin' upstairs.

Mrs Purkiss If you could 'ave waited a couple of months, yer dad would 'ave been out of the clink.

Winnie Never mind, 'e'll be in time for the christenin'.

Polly notices Jessie with Joe, as Jessie gives a saucy laugh

Polly Hey, Jessie—'ere, I want yer.

Jessie I'm busy.

Polly I know, that's why I want yer.

Polly goes and pulls Jessie away from Joe

Joe Nark it, Poll, don't spoil me fun.

Jessie What's the matter wiv you?

Polly You never give up, do yer?

Jessie What business is it of yours?

Polly Kate's my mate—so lay orf.

Jessie is about to return to Joe

   Kate enters

Polly decides against it

Joe Where you bin, leavin' me stuck 'ere like some fourpenny 'ambone?

Kate seems disturbed

   What's up, Kate?

Kate I just took a bit of weddin' cake up to young Rosy Potter. She couldn't eat it, Joe—she can't eat anymore. All 'er jaw—it's 'orrible.

Joe takes her into his arms

Joe Now, come on—this is Win's wedding day. Blimey you seen phossy jaw before.

Some of the Guests gather round Kate and Joe

(*sotto voce*) Pull yerself togevver—people are lookin'. There's nuffin' you can do about it.

Kate breaks away in anger

Kate There is somethin' we can do about it—there must be.

Joe (*in a temper*) Look, will you give up, just for today! This is a weddin', not a wake!

Dot comes running in, waving a copy of "The Link"

Dot 'Ere, we're in the paper.

Polly What paper?

Dot *The Link*. Mrs Besant's writ about us. Kate, come and read it.

Kate goes and takes the paper

Kate (*reading*) "Today I saw 'orror. In a match factory in London's East End . . ."

Joe goes and snatches the paper from Kate

Joe What good do you think this is goin' to do yer? An article written by a woman who's the laughing stock of London—in a paper nobody's ever 'eard of.

Maggie It's a beginnin'.

Joe Beginnin'? Of what? More trouble—ain't we got enough trouble down 'ere?

Kate Give me that paper!

Joe You'll curse the day you ever met that Besant woman—and don't forget I warned yer!

Kate Give me that paper!

Joe throws the paper back to Kate. Mrs Purkiss intervenes

Mrs Purkiss Now now, you two—stop fightin'—just for today.

Old Min Come on, everybody, what about a toast to the bride and groom.

(*She sings*)

   MUSIC: MIND YOU, BERT

   There they are
   The 'appy couple,
   Beginning the great adventure

                    A journey together
                    Through all kinds of weather
Perce Don't make such a noise, Min, you'll wake the baby.
Old Min May you find 'appiness.
Polly When yer do let us in on it.
Docker Don't forget to take yer boots off Bert!
Old Min (*singing*) Just think
                            The laughter and tears
                            The joys and the fears
Men   In uvver words, Bert,
                            You're in it,
                            You're in it right up to your ears.
Docker   'Ere's to you, mud in yer eye
                            Cheerio, never say die
                            Now your spliced,
                            'Ere's wishin' you all the best!
                            'Ere's to you, skin off yer nose
                            Bottoms up, keep on yer toes
                            Marriage is nice
                            And it's cheap at the price
                            For two can live cheaper than one.
Maggie   Mind you, Bert,
                            Being wed ain't always milk and honey,
                            Like fer instance when yer short of money—
                            No more mates to spend a boozey night wiv
                            Still now you got a missus you can fight wiv.
All   'Ere's to you, mud in yer eye,
                            Cheerio, never say die
                            Now you're spliced
                            'Ere's wishin' you all the best
                            'Ere's to you, skin off yer nose
                            Bottoms up, keep on yer toes
                            Marriage is nice, and it's cheap at the price,
                            For two can live cheaper than one.
Docker   Mind you, Bert,
                            Bein' wed at first is all romantic,
                            But comes a time it drives yer nearly frantic
                            Married bliss is something that you read of—
                            But when you're wed it's something you're in need of.
All   'Ere's to you, etc.
Docker   Mind you, Bert,
                            Being spliced ain't always lovey dovey,
                            Soon she'll start "You never really loved me"
                            Say I love you, and she'll say you're lyin'
                            But then take cover 'cause the plates start flyin'
All   'Ere's to you, etc.
Mrs Purkiss   Mind you, Bert,
                            Just remember love is there for livin'

If you can learn the takin' and the giving,
Take no notice how these others keep on,
'Cause now you've got a back to warm your feet on.

All   'Ere's to you, etc.

*Everyone dances a "Knees Up" routine, then dances off as the Lights
slowly fade to a Black-out*

SCENE 5

Under a Street Lamp

The music changes to

DEAR LADY

Under the light of the street lamp Kate sits writing to Annie

Kate (*speaking*)   My dear lady,
We thank you very much for your kind interest that
you have taken in us poor girls and hope that you will
succeed in your undertaking.

*A Light picks out Annie, who stands reading the letter by a small table on
the opposite side of the stage*

Annie (*speaking*)   Dear lady,
They have been trying to get us poor girls to say that
it is all lies that has been printed.

(*singing*)   And trying to make us sign papers
That it is all lies . . .

Kate (*speaking*)   Dear lady,
Nobody knows what it is we have to put up with, 'cause
we will not sign them.

(*singing*)   We all thank you very much
For the kindness you have shown to us . . .

Annie (*singing*)   Dear lady,
We hope that you will not get into any trouble, on our
behalf,
as what you have spoken is quite true . . .

Kate (*singing*)   Dear lady,
We hope that if there will be any meeting
you will let us know it in the book.
I have no more to say at the present,
From yours truly . . .

Annie ⎫   With kind friends wishes for you, dear lady,
Kate ⎭   For the kind love you have shown us girls.

The Light fades on Kate

The Office of the Freethought Bookshop

The Lights come up on a small room at the rear of the premises. Seated at a small table checking accounts is Paula Westerby, a pretty, well-dressed young woman. Annie stands in thought as she folds the letter

Paula What do the girls have to say?

Annie The management are putting on the pressure since my article in *The Link*, they're trying to . . .

Annie is interrupted by the entrance of the young Bernard Shaw

Shaw Am I interrupting something—like a cup of tea?

Annie You're too late.

Paula How are you, George?

Shaw I'm not sure, Paula, trying to get through that shop out there is quite a hazard.

Annie Perhaps one day you'll give us a hand to tidy up.

Shaw Annie, would you say that these pamphlets that I write to enlighten the working class as to their plight have some effect?

Annie I know they do.

Shaw Then don't you think they might at least be displayed so that unsuspecting converts can peruse them?

Annie When we can afford a paid staff—

Shaw Heavens, woman, all we need is a bigger shop!

Annie —and when we can afford a bigger shop!

Paula Now, now, you two. I'm trying to perform a miracle with the little money we have.

Shaw Try the loaves and fishes?

Annie What did you think of my article about the "Matchgirls"?

Shaw Very good, though I must admit to reservations about the dénouement.

Annie What do you mean?

Shaw A little melodramatic don't you think?

Annie Everything I said in that article was true.

Shaw (*taking a copy of "The Link" from his pocket*) I'm not disputing that— but this last paragraph . . . (*He reads*) "Country clergymen with shares in this match factory, draw down on your knees your daughters and pass your hand tenderly over the silky clustering curls and thank heaven for your large dividend and the fact that your daughters don't have to live like these matchgirls." It sounds like *East Lynne* written by the editor of the *Financial Times*.

Annie is furious, and sweeps out of the office

Shaw Paula, what have I said wrong this time?

Paula Have you no tact . . .

Shaw Tact has never been a strong point with the Irish. It comes from years of trying to cope with the British.

Paula Don't you see she was getting back at her husband?
Shaw The Reverend Frank Besant, I didn't know he was a shareholder.
Paula And she misses her daughter very much.

Annie returns, reading a telegram

I thought it was my job to open the post.
Annie This is a telegram.
Shaw A telegram no less. Fame at last.
Annie (*referring to the telegram*) Wonderful—wonderful. Just what we want.
Paula You mean someone has sent us a donation?
Annie (*reading*) Listen to this—"Letter to hand this morning. Nothing but a tissue of lies. Your article will receive legal attention." (*She hands the telegram to Shaw*) Let them—just let those directors sue me. That's the kind of publicity we need for these matchgirls. We must get the press behind this—what response have we had so far?
Paula Not very much. The *Pall Mall Gazette* and the *Star* have asked for details. How did these directors get hold of a copy of *The Link*?
Annie I sent them one.

Shaw hugs Annie

Shaw Annie, you're wonderful.
Annie We must do something to get this campaign moving.
Paula We're doing all we can.
Annie What about *The Times*?
Shaw You don't expect *The Times* to get excited over working conditions? And women's working conditions at that.
Annie What about the London Trades Council?
Paula We could try—but they've got enough trouble with the gas workers and the tram workers—
Shaw —and the dockers!
Annie (*annoyed*) Why are you always such a Job's comforter?
Shaw Annie, we have got to face the fact that it is going to be very difficult to capture the attention of the public over these matchgirls. After all, I don't suppose general working conditions there are any worse than anywhere else.
Annie (*with temper*) No! What about the fines, the stoppages, the wages— and what about phossy jaw?
Shaw Annie, I am on your side.
Annie These girls have no way of airing their grievances—no way at all— they're completely helpless.

During the latter part of this conversation a noise develops, as the Girls are heard singing and yelling "Strike"

Paula goes to see

Shaw Good heavens, what's all that noise?

Paula rushes in

Paula Annie, the matchgirls, they've . . .

*Before Paula can get any further the Girls, led by Kate, pour in. They are
excited, some almost hysterical as they mill round the office, pushing and
shoving, jumping on the chairs*

Annie (*shouting above the din*) Kate, what is all this?
Kate We're on strike!
Girls We're on strike!

*The chanting of the word "strike" almost forms a background to the first
part of this conversation*

Winnie Yus, there's thousands more in the street.
Louie They're holdin' up the traffic.
Annie But you can't strike, how can you?
Maggie It's easy. You just stop what you're doing . . .
Polly Stuff two fingers up the foreman's nose . . .
Girls And walk out.
Kate We want you to help us like you promised.
Shaw Help you? Trying to get publicity, trying to get you organized—
that's one thing. But a strike . . . Do you realize what you've done?
Who's ever heard of women going on strike?
Kate (*angrily*) What 'ave you 'eard—what do you know. You sit 'ere
sellin' yer books on 'ow to put fings right—but what do yer know? (*She
grabs Louie*) Look at 'er. 'Ave you ever 'eard or seen anythin' like that?

Kate whips the shawl from Louie's head, revealing a large bald patch

She got that from carryin' 'eavy trays on 'er 'ead. D'yer know 'ow old
she is—twelve—the ripe old age of twelve.
Louie (*breaking away*) You rotten cow—doin' that to me—lettin' 'em see.

Louie runs out, crying

Shaw (*shocked*) I'm sorry—I didn't mean to . . .
Kate What did you mean? (*She looks at Annie, then moves to the door*)
Come on, we can fight this on our own.
Annie Kate, come back . . .
Kate Why did yer promise to 'elp us?
Annie Kate, come back . . .
Kate We're used to broken promises—come on, all of yer.
Annie KATE!!

The two firebrands face each other

Annie What did you do to your arm?
Mrs Purkiss She cut it at the unveilin'. She climbed up on the statue of
Gladstone—
Winnie —and cut 'er arm, on purpose—
Maggie —and she let the blood run down the statue.
Shaw (*amazed*) But why? Why do a thing like that? I mean, what were
you trying to prove?

Suddenly Annie is enthusiastic. Kate did just what she would have done

Annie That they have more guts than the dockers and the tram-workers put together. This, by the way, girls, is Bernard Shaw—he really is on our side.

Some of the Girls giggle and nudge each other

Now, tell me about this strike.

All the Girls speak at once

Now wait—wait. Kate, tell me.

Kate It was like I told yer in my letter. They was tryin' to get us to sign this paper, sayin' what you'd printed in *The Link* wasn't true—

Old Min —and we told 'em what to do wiv the paper.

Kate Then the foreman kept pickin' on me—always findin' fault.

Beattie Made 'er life a bloody misery.

Kate In the end they found some excuse to sack me.

Winnie And when Kate walked out, so did we.

Mrs Purkiss It spread like wildfire—they come out in their 'undreds. You go and 'ave a look out in the street—there's a mile of 'em out there.

Old Min They're 'oldin' up the traffic.

Annie (*excitedly*) Very well, they want a fight—we'll give them one.

MUSIC: WE'RE GONNA SHOW 'EM

Shaw exits

Kate
We know the way now—
Here we come!
It's from today, now—
Here we come.
We will set the Thames alight tonight,
From here to Tilbury!

Kate **Annie** ⎱	We're gonna show 'em—	{ (*Singing together*)
Girls	Now we know!	
Kate **Annie** ⎱	We're gonna show 'em—	{ (*Singing together*)
Girls	Here we go!	
All	Show 'em that We're just not takin' no more! It's us from now on.	

The girls exit as the music continues

SCENE 7

On the way to Parliament

The Girls, led by Annie, cross the stage, still singing. Kate follows up in the rear. In the shadows, Joe is waiting. He pulls Kate from the march

Joe Kate, I wanna talk to yer.

Kate (*impatiently*) Not now, Joe, we're marchin' to the 'Ouse of Commons
—imagine us in Parliament!

Joe This is important.

Kate So is this—we're on strike, we . . .

Joe (*angrily*) Will you listen a minute, this is important—it's about us—
you and me.

Kate Well, 'urry up then.

Joe My Uncle George came down today from Bradford, 'e's sold 'is shop,
'e's goin' to emigrate to America.

Kate What's that got to do wiv us?

Joe 'E wants me to go wiv 'im, start a business over there. Will yer come,
Kate? Let's get married.

The full implication of Joe's last remark slowly gets home to Kate

The Girls appear again

Winnie Come on, Kate, we want you to lead us!

Joe Let's start a new life together—what d'yer say?

Kate But why do we 'ave to talk about it now?

Winnie Come on, Kate.

Joe Because it's important.

Winnie Kate!

Joe There ain't much time—'e's goin' next week.

Kate But, Joe, you just can't pick up yer tracks like that.

Joe Why not? There's just you and me.

Winnie Kate, come and lead us.

Joe Will yer come?

Winnie Kate!

Kate I dunno, Joe, I dunno . . .

Winnie Kate!

Kate All right, I'm comin'. (*She joins Winnie*) I love yer, Joe, I do love
yer . . .

MUSIC: WE'RE GONNA SHOW 'EM (*reprise*)

Girls	We're gonna show 'em—
	They're gonna get a surprise!
	They better run for their lives
	Run for their lives!
	Or they're gonna get a surprise—
	We're gonna show 'em!
	That we ain't takin' no more.
	They've gone a little too far
	Little too far
	Now we're gonna show who we are!
Polly	What a lark!
Maggie	What a caper!
Dot ⎫	You can read
Win ⎭	In yer paper—

⎰ (*Singing*
⎱ *together*)

Kate   What a do
                        What an uproar.

All   From now on we're gonna show 'em
                        We don't take no more!
                        We're gonna show 'em
                        Clear the way.
                        We're gonna show 'em
                        It's today
                        That we're goin' to set the Thames alight
                        From here to Tilbury!

                        We're gonna show 'em!
                        They're gonna get a surprise!
                        They better run for their lives
                        Run for their lives
                        Or they're gonna get a surprise!
                        We're gonna show 'em—
                        That we ain't takin' no more!
                        They've gone a little too far
                        Little too far,
                        Now we're gonna show who we are!

Girls   What a lark,
                        What a caper!
                        You can read
                        In your paper.
                        What a do
                        What an uproar!

Girls   From now on we're gonna show 'em—
                        We don't take no more!
                        We're gonna show 'em
                        Clear the way!
                        We're gonna show 'em
                        It's the day!
                        When we show that we ain't taking no more,
                        We're on our way now!
                        We're gonna show 'em—
                        We're gonna show 'em—
                        We're gonna show 'em—

(Shouting)   WE'RE GONNA SHOW 'EM!!

                              CURTAIN

ACT II

Hope Court. One week later

Music. It is a hot June afternoon. A group of Girls sits around dejectedly. Louie is bouncing a ball as she plaintively sings "Phossy Jaw"

Old Min We should never 'ave done it.
Louie I'm 'ungry.
Mrs Purkiss Go down the Salvation Army and get some free soup.
Louie I don't like soup. (*She continues singing*)
    Top-grade selectable
    Hardly detectable
    Phosphorus, phosphorus . . .
Winnie Ain't it 'ot.
Jessie Where's this money, this Besant woman promised us? Stop bouncin' that ball!
Louie I'm 'ungry.
Mrs Purkiss Kate's gorn up to see Mrs Besant today.
Jessie Kate's always seein' Mrs Besant.
Old Min They're bringin' girls down from Glasgow.
Winnie (*holding her full stomach in pain*) I must feed this kid.
Old Min Some of 'em 'ave started to go back.
Mrs Purkiss And there's plenty that ain't.
Jessie Stop bouncin' that ball.

Jessie goes to Louie, pushes her, grabs the ball and throws it off

Louie I'm 'ungry.

    Louie runs off crying. She charges into Polly who enters carrying suitcases, pots, pans and other domestic articles

Polly 'Ere, why don't yer look where I'm goin'? Any of you see Beattie or Nell?
Old Min What are you doin', moving 'ome?
Polly No, we're goin' 'oppin'.
Mrs Purkiss Kate says we should stick together.
Polly Listen, we been out on strike for over a week now—what's 'appened? Nothin' . . .
Old Min We're in the papers every day.
Winnie They started a fund, we're goin' to get some money soon.
Polly Well, I can't wait, I wanna eat—now. And there's two ways a matchgirl can do that at the minute—and I'm tryin' hop pickin' first.

Beattie and Nell struggle on with their cases and odd impediments

Come on, you two. Where yer been?
Nell I dunno, what's my old lady goin' to say when she finds I got all this!
Beattie 'Ow we gonna get it all down there?
Polly Joe's gonna lend us his barrer.
Beattie But why did we have to bring all this stuff?

MUSIC: COCKNEY SPARRERS

Polly (*speaking*) 'Cause you sleeps in a shed,
And it don't arf get cold,
Sanitation consists of
A hole with a pole.
There's all kinds of creepies
That crawls up the wall,
And no matter which way you turn
There's positively, absolutely,
Quite definitely,
No view at all!

Beattie
Nell } No view?   { (*speaking together*)
Polly No winders.
Beattie
Nell } Oh, blimey.   { (*speaking together*)
Polly (*singing*) But—
We'll arrange our bits and pieces,
And you'll never want to roam
With a knicknack 'ere,
And a knicknack there,
It'll be like 'ome from 'ome—
Beattie
Nell
Polly } We packed our bags,   { (*singing together*)
Put on our glad rags
We've harnessed up the moke—
Beattie
Nell } We've had a barf—   { (*singing together*)
Polly Just 'arf and 'arf—
We gonna leave the smoke.
Beattie
Nell
Polly } We're cockney sparrers,   { (*singing together*)
Wiv our barrers,
Off to take a ride!
Beattie No more room inside.
Beattie
Nell
Polly } Till we get out in the countryside. { (*singing together*)
Nell I've ironed me skirt—
Beattie I've shook me fur
To empty out the moth!
Polly A packet of lozenges in me bag—

<table>
<tr><td>Nel!</td><td>This fresh air makes me cough!
Oh, the landed gentry are going to be in for a fright
When these cockney sparrers arrive
With their barrers tonight . . .</td></tr>
</table>

Joe enters pushing a hand-cart

The music continues

Joe All right, 'ere's yer barrer.

Polly rushes to Joe, flings her arms around him

Polly Oh, you luverly, Joe, you remembered.

Joe (*seeing the luggage*) 'Ow you gonna get all that stuff on there?

Polly Don't worry, Joe—we'll manage.

Joe Go careful with that barrer—I use it for my pigeons.

Beattie (*looking in the barrow*) I can see that.

Polly Well, come on, you two, don't stand there, pile up the barrer!

Joe surveys the piled-up barrow

Joe You sure you ain't forgot nuffin'?

More Girls and Dockers enter

They dance as they sing the following

Polly	Like what?
Joe	A chiffonnière.
Old Min	A barrel of beer.
Winnie	'Ere, borrow me mum's "whatnot".
Docker	A jubilee mug—
Docker	A leopard skin rug—
Nell	There's something that we forgot—
All	A bunch of limey's, Oh cor blimeys On the frog and toad—

Beattie **Nell** **Polly**	We'll hold up the road Whenever they see our peculiar load—	*(singing together)*
A Docker	Some table ware—	
A Docker	A rocking chair—	
A Docker	A stool to rest yer feet.	
Joe	A fryin' pan—	
Polly	I've brought me fan— You never know who you'll meet!	
Beattie	The sap's gonna rise in some fam'ly trees all right When these Cockney sparrers arrive with their barrers tonight!	

Louie rushes on with her case

Louie Poll, Poll—can I come?

Polly No, you're too young.

Louie Nobody's ever worried about that before. Let me come, Poll.

Nell (*to Polly, sotto voce*) Let 'er come—the cookin'—she can do all the cookin'.

Polly (*twigging*) Yes, all right, Louie—you can come. Put yer stuff on the . . .

Polly sees the cart is piled high, and there are several objects on the ground. She picks them up and piles them on to Louie, who seems to disappear under the load

Polly There yer are, Joe, I told yer we'd manage. Right, that's the lot.

A Docker   Wait—you forgot
                    Yer ironing board,

A Docker   An 'arpsichord,
                    To play a sweet gavotte.

Polly dances

A Docker   A pair of horns,

A Docker   A bowl for yer corns—

Mrs Purkiss And a very essential pot!

A Docker dances

All   Yus, the landed gentry
                    Are gonna be in for a fright!
                    When these Cockney sparrers arrive
                    With their barrers tonight!

                    La la lala lala—
                    La la woops er daisy—
                    Come on, don't be lazy—

                    When these Cockney sparrers arrive
                    With their barrers tonight!

Maggie enters, almost carrying Dot. They are both very dishevelled. Blood trickles from a cut on Dot's forehead

Maggie Give me an 'and.

Joe goes quickly to Maggie, takes Dot and lays her gently on the ground. The Girls crowd round

Joe Stand back, give 'er some air. Somebody get some water.

Winnie goes off

Mrs Purkiss Maggie, what 'appened?

Kate enters, excited

Kate 'Ere, I saw Mrs Besant . . . (*She surveys the scene*) What's 'appened? What's goin' on? (*She joins Joe*)

Mrs Purkiss That's just what I asked 'er.

Kate What's 'appened, Maggie, what's 'appened?

Winnie returns with a cup of water

Maggie We was on picket at the factory, some of these Glasgow whores turned up. We tried to talk to 'em—but it wasn't no good. They tried to go into the factory, and we tried to stop 'em.

Joe makes Dot take a drink of water

Joe Come on now, take a drink of this.

Dot gives a moan as she does so

Jessie 'Ow is she, Joe?

Joe She'll do. She's 'ad a boot or two in the ribs, but she'll do. I should get her orf 'ome.

Mrs Purkiss Take 'er up to my place.

Winnie and another Girl help Dot off

Joe Well, it certainly looks as though you're winnin'. You know a lot of 'em 'ave started to go back.

Kate (*angrily*) We know.

Joe All right, I was only tellin' yer.

Kate We don't need yer to tell us. We ain't goin' back—are we?

The Girls agree half-heartedly

Mrs Purkiss All right, come on all of yer. Let's go and picket the factory' and Gawd 'elp any of them Glasgow cows if they try anyfing wiv me.

Kate Don't start any more trouble.

Jessie I don't want to go up the factory.

Mrs Purkiss (*looking at Joe*) You never give up do yer.

Mrs Purkiss pushes the reluctant Jessie off in front of her; most of the others follow, including Polly

Beattie Where you goin'?

Polly Up the factory.

Nell Ain't we goin' "oppin"?

Polly You 'eard the call to arms, didn't yer? The Scots are invadin' again. Thanks for the barrer, Joe.

Joe Hey, wait a minute, what am I supposed to do with all this stuff?

Polly Stick it up yer—pigeon loft. Don't worry, I'll pick it up later. Come on you two.

Polly, Nell and Beattie exit

Joe and Kate are left alone

Kate What you doin' around this time of day? Why ain't yer workin'?

Joe I got the sack yesterday.

Kate The sack? Why didn't yer tell me?

Joe 'Cause I didn't see yer yesterday, or the day before. I've hardly set eyes on you since this strike started.

Kate I'm sorry Joe, but—well, you know 'ow it is.

Joe No I don't know 'ow it is. I don't know 'ow a girl can say she belongs to a feller . . .

Kate Joe—don't let's start a row.

Joe (*loudly*) I ain't startin' a row.

Kate (*more loudly*) You are startin' a row! (*quietly*) You are startin' a row. That's 'ow rows start by people shoutin' at each other.

Joe (*smiling*) Blimey, we should know, we've 'ad enough practice.

Kate 'Ow did you get the sack? I thought you 'ad the foreman fixed wiv the dropsie.

Joe So did I. But it wasn't enough. 'E wanted a bit more, then a bit more every week. So Saturday I sees him in the *Anchor*, like always he 'olds out 'is hand, and I "grease" it. Then 'e looks at what I give 'im, then he looks at me and 'e says, "It ain't enough, Joey boy, not for 'avin' a reg'lar ticket, I want a bit more". So I give it to 'im—right between the eyes.

Kate You mean you 'it 'im?!

Joe 'E sailed across that bar room floor like a boat in full sail.

Kate laughs with the sheer joy

Kate Oh 'ow lovely, to be able to 'it yer foreman. That would be better than a day at Sarfend.

Joe Never mind about Sarfend. What about America, Kate?

Kate I've thought about it Joe. I've never stopped thinkin' about it.

Joe Thinkin' ain't enough.

MUSIC: COMES A TIME

(*singing*)	It 'as to be now, it 'as to be now.
(*speaking*)	You can't keep dodgin' round corners all yer life.
	Comes a time
	When you know that the moment is now
	To make up your mind, to leave all behind
	To go . . .
Kate (*singing*)	Yet you know,
	Comes a time—
	How will you know which road is the one?
	Your head tells you stay
	Your heart, go away today.
Joe	No-one else can guide you,
	Run away and hide you
	Still must face the truth someday.
Both	Comes a time,
	And you know that the moment is now—
	To know where you're going,
	And knowing—

To say—
I will.

At the end of the song Joe and Kate are about to kiss when Annie enters and spoils the moment, much to Joe's disgust

Annie Ah there you are, Kate. Good evening, Joe—it's a nice evening.
Joe It was.
Annie Kate, I was hoping that we might . . .
Joe Bit dangerous for you ain't it, Mrs Besant? Wanderin' around dockland all alone?
Annie I come down to the docks alone very often.
Joe I know, but never at this 'our.
Kate Joe!
Joe When a docker's 'ungry he'll listen. But at night when 'e's got a few pints inside 'im, you better hang on to your stays.
Kate Joe!
Annie Can I have a word with you Kate—alone?
Joe Not before I've 'ad a word wiv you. (*He points to Kate*) She's virgin soil for you, ain't she—green pastures. I've known 'er ever since she was a kid. Wherever there was a fight goin' she was in—wiv 'er 'ead down. But I'm tellin' you, the day she marries me . . .
Kate 'Oo said I was goin' ter marry you?!
Joe Keep out of this, it's got nuffin' to do wiv you. (*To Annie*) The day she marries me she'll walk down the aisle carryin' a banner. But it'll be for us—'er and me—that's the only cause we're gonna fight for.
Annie (*angrily*) But don't you see you can't do it on your own!
Joe I've seen you, Mrs Besant, hold a thousand men spellbound down at them dock gates. But I've 'eard you've never been able to 'old one man in yer life.
Annie I'll see you tomorrow, Kate.

Annie stalks off in anger

Kate (*to Joe*) Oh you—you—you docker, you! Now look what you've done!
Joe What I've done!!

Kate rushes off after Annie

Kate (*calling*) Wait fer me, dear lady—wait fer me . . .
Joe (*calling after her*) I'm warnin' yer!

MUSIC: COMES A TIME (*reprise*)

Joe No-one else can guide you,
Run away and hide you—
Still must face the truth some day.
Comes a time
When you know that the moment is now—
That moment of loneliness—
Time standing still—

Your life in your hands is suspended until
You know where you're going,
And knowing—
You say—"I will".

SCENE 2

The drawing-room of Annie's house, St John's Wood

The room is indicated by a decorative screen in front of which is set a small table with tea. Shaw and Annie are seated, the latter perusing the day's newspapers

Annie A complete boycott—not a word.

Shaw The *Star* and the *Pall Mall Gazette* carried it yesterday—they've launched your Strike Fund.

Annie It's not enough.

Shaw Patience, Annie, patience.

Annie We don't have time!

Shaw You don't expect the Tory press to be interested in a story like this do you? A bunch of girls on strike in the East End of London . . .

Annie There are more than two thousand girls . . .

Shaw Industry for *The Times* begins and ends at the Stock Exchange.

Annie But nothing is happening! We just hold meetings. The crowds applaud—and then go home.

Shaw They've seen it all before.

Annie What do you mean by that?

Shaw It's always the same old faces. You, me, Eleanor Marx, Aveling, etc. We're the maniacs, the radicals, God's gift to the music hall comedian. But if we could get one of those girls to stand up for five minutes, and tell her own story, in her own words, it would mean more than all the speeches the rest of us could make put together.

Annie (*after a pause*) It's a brilliant idea, George. (*She kisses him lightly*) You're a genius.

Shaw I know. I'm leaving it to posterity. Tell me how did you get on with Mr Theodore Bryant and his fellow Directors?

Annie They just sat like ostriches, burying their heads in the sand denying everything.

Shaw (*referring to a newspaper*) But damn it all woman, this article here by Llewellyn Smith.

Annie They deny it.

Shaw But he's an accountant. They agreed to let him examine their books. (*Reading from his newspaper*) "I can find no figures to support the Directors' statement that there is an average wage of eleven shillings a week." Damn it all, these are facts.

Annie They deny everything, the fines, the stoppages.

Shaw Do these people really know what goes on in their factory?

Annie I doubt it. Do you know what they call phossy jaw? An occupational hazard. "This is just another of your political stunts, ma'am," one of them shouted at me.

Shaw A strike is politics, or it should be.

There is a knock at the front door. Annie is engrossed in her newspaper

There's a knock at the front door.

Annie does not reply

Don't worry, I'll go.

Shaw exits

Annie remains with her paper

After a few moments Shaw returns, followed by Kate in her best clothes

We have a surprise visitor.

Annie Kate! What brings you up here, and on a Sunday?

Kate I 'ad to see yer, Mrs Besant.

Shaw How did you get up here?

Kate The conductors are giving all the matchgirls free rides on the trams down the East End. I got up to Aldgate then walked the rest.

Shaw From Aldgate—that's miles!

Kate It's lovely up here. I walked over 'Ampstead 'Eath. I never knew there was so much sky.

Annie Sit down and have some tea, you must be exhausted.

Kate Ta.

Shaw offers his chair, Annie pours tea. Shaw offers a sandwich. Kate takes one—very daintily

Shaw That won't fill a tooth, take the plate.

Rather embarrassed, Kate does so and for the rest of the scene wrestles with tea, sandwiches and table napkin

Annie How are the girls?

Kate All right—I suppose.

Shaw You must remember you've made history. No-one's ever heard of women going on strike before.

Kate We get 'ungry though, just the same as the men.

Annie The Strike Fund has been launched, you'll have some money soon. It may not be much, but it will help. Have you had a Committee meeting to draw up your demands?

Kate That's what I come to see yer about. I don't know 'ow to run a meetin'—they all shout at once.

Shaw That's quite normal.

Kate I can't 'ear them—they can't 'ear me. Then I say all them in favour to put up their 'ands, and they do.

Annie Well?

Kate Then I say all those against—and they all put their 'ands up again.

Shaw This smells of democracy.

Kate And it always ends up in a row.

Annie I have a little book on meeting procedure you can have. I found it a great help.

Shaw And she has the scars to prove it.

Annie (*after a pause*) Do you remember the first time we met, Kate?

Kate (*with hero-worship*) I'll never forget.

Annie Do you remember the way you described working in that factory to me?

Kate (*after a pause*) Not really. I just say the first fing what comes into my 'ead. Joe says that's my trouble.

Annie Do you think you could stand up in front of a hundred, maybe a thousand people and tell them the story—in the same way?

Kate 'Ow do yer mean?

Annie Tell them like you told me. Tell them what you want.

Kate (*laughing*) Me? I'd be scared stiff.

Annie If the others were with you?

Kate But I wouldn't know what to do—what to say.

Annie We'd help you.

Shaw We've got to let people know about you.

Kate Everybody knows in the East End . . .

Shaw It isn't enough, Kate.

Annie Would you try?

Kate (*after a pause*) Would you be there?

Annie All the time.

Kate But it's daft, me talkin' at a meetin'. Everybody would laugh.

Annie We'll see.

The music introduction to THIS LIFE OF MINE begins, as the Lights fade

SCENE 3

A Meeting

A Light picks out Kate on a platform. On either side of her are Annie and Shaw. The Matchgirls and Dockers lend support with their various placards, which read:

SUPPORT THE MATCHGIRLS
DIRECTORS ACCUSED OF CONTRAVENING THE TRUCK ACT
THE MATCHGIRLS' FIGHT IS YOUR FIGHT
TRADES UNION CONGRESS APPROACHED
BRADLAUGH M.P. QUESTIONS HOME SECRETARY
DOCKERS LEADER PLEDGES SUPPORT
MATCHGIRLS RECEIVE FIRST STRIKE PAY

MUSIC: THIS LIFE OF MINE

Kate Ever since the day that I was born
There's always been someone telling us

What to do, and this and that and when,
With my three-score years and ten.

Kate   This is my life—
Only I can live it,
And from now on I'm gonna say
What I'm gonna do with it.

With this life of mine
Maybe I'll change a thing or two,
Have a fling or two—
I know where I am going to
With this life of mine
Want to have my say.
Maybe I'll have to yell and shout
I'll be in, not out,
I'll show 'em what it's all about
With this life of mine.

Girls   I want to clear the air,
See just where I'm going.
Life is for living, and
From now my cup's gonna be overflowing.

Kate   With this life of mine
I'll try and find the truth somehow
Not tomorrow, now
When I take my bow
With this life of mine.

Dockers	Kate and Girls
I want to clear the air	I want to clear the air
See just where I'm going	See just where I'm going
Life is for living	Life is for living, and—
From now my cup's gonna be overflowin'	From now my cup's gonna be overflowin'
	With this life of mine I'll try and find the truth somehow
When I take my bow	Not tomorrow now!
With this life of mine	When I take my bow
With this life of mine	With this life of mine
With this life of mine	With this life of mine
	This life of mine

The music continues quietly as the Lights fade

SCENE 4

Down by the Docks. Night

Jessie stands alone under a street lamp. A ship's siren sounds. Joe enters

Joe You seen Kate?
Jessie She's wiv Mrs Besant I expect.
Joe At this time of night?
Jessie Well she's famous now ain't she? Gets 'er name in the papers—spoutin' at all these meetin's—silly cow. Blimey, if I 'ad the chance that she's got.
Joe What are you talkin' about?
Jessie Goin' to America wiv you. Cor, if I 'ad a chance like that you wouldn't see me for dust.
Joe (*after a pause*) So you'd come to America wiv me, would yer?
Jessie Wiv you—wiv anybody. Anyfing to get out of this stinkin' 'ole.
Joe Oh, I see. I thought it might 'ave been me.
Jessie It might be.
Joe If you looked at another man when we got out there—I'd break . . .
Jessie You'd never 'ave to worry about me. If I went wiv yer, I'd work for yer, I'd slave for yer—and only you.
Joe (*smiling*) I could stay at 'ome then, could I? Put me feet up.
Jessie If you wanted to. (*after a pause*) But you wouldn't because you ain't that sort of bloke.
Joe The question is, are you that sort of girl—that you say you are?
Jessie That's a chance you'd 'ave to take. Unless you take my word.
Joe Act in haste, repent at leisure. That's what they say.
Jessie 'Ow would you know. You've only ever 'ad one girl in yer life.
Joe Kate and me grew up together, seemed natural like.
Jessie It don't seem natural to me—the way she's acting now.
Joe (*unsure*) You know Kate.
Jessie That's no excuse. Not if you belong to a bloke.
Joe She never looks at another feller.
Jessie Neither would I.

Joe is silent. A ship's siren is heard

Joe You're putting ideas in my 'ead.
Jessie That'll be the day. (*after a pause*) Do you want me to give Kate a message?

Kate emerges from the shadows

Kate You don't 'ave to bother, I'm 'ere.

Jessie makes to move off

Jessie G'night, Joe.
Joe Where yer goin', Jess, stay 'ere.
Jessie But, Joe . . .
Joe I said stay 'ere!

Jessie remains

Kate What's goin' on?
Joe 'Ow should I know, you tell me.
Kate What's she doin' 'ere?

Joe She lives round 'ere, or don't you remember.

Kate (*wearily*) Joe, don't start that again, you know I've been at a meetin'.

Joe I wonder you don't live up there with Mrs Besant.

Kate It's important!

Joe Is it? What am I supposed to do? Sit around and play tiddly-winks?

Kate I know you better than that.

Joe Well, 'ere's somethin' you don't know. I'm sailin' for America on Friday.

Kate On Friday!

Joe Now I can take you, I can go alone—or I can take somebody else.

Kate (*looking at Jessie*) I needn't ask who the somebody else is.

Joe It makes no difference. No more words, no more arguments . . .

Kate But Joe, you know . . .

Joe I don't know anything, and I don't care any more. Just make up yer mind—this strike or me. (*After a pause*) Can I buy yer a drink down the *Anchor*?

Kate is silent

All right, come on, Jess. (*To Kate*) Remember—Friday.

Joe and Jess exit

Kate stands alone. Joe and Jessie are heard singing, off

Jessie ⎫ Comes a time
Joe ⎭ When you know that the moment is now— ⎰ (*off, singing*)
That moment of loneliness—
Time standing still.
Your life in your hands is suspended, until
You know where you're going, and knowing,
You say "I will".

The Lights fade

SCENE 5

Hope Court. Morning, two days later

The Committee—Winnie, Mrs Purkiss, Polly and Maggie are in session, while Old Min squats holding a board which reads "COMMITEA MEETING—BELT UP". Dot and Beattie stand observing the uproar as the Committee argue among themselves

Mrs Purkiss Quiet! Quiet, all of yer! Will you shut your gobs—SHUT UP!

There is quiet

Cor blimey, it's like feedin' time at the Zoo.

Old Min They should be so lucky.

Mrs Purkiss Polly!
Polly Chairman, if you please.
Winnie Then get on wiv it.
Polly (*reading from a book*) Now it says 'ere. "The duties of a Chairman are to maintain order . . ."
Mrs Purkiss Oh put that book of Mrs Besant's away!
Polly Order h'if you please. (*Back to her book*) ". . . and to see that due respect is paid to the Chair."

Maggie gives her the "razz"

"To rule promptly on questions of order. The Chairman should always be of good appearance, all beards and moustaches should be well trimmed."
Winnie You need a shave.

The others laugh

Polly You're out of order, Win.
Old Min She's been like that for the last nine months.

Beattie wanders on

Mrs Purkiss I wish Kate was 'ere, she'd do it proper.
Polly Well, she ain't is she, so I'm doin' it while she's busy.
Beattie Where is Kate?
Maggie I dunno.
Winnie I never saw 'er at all yesterday.
Beattie She ain't deserted us, 'as she?
Polly Kate would never do that!
Beattie Joe's goin' to America, ain't he?
Mrs Purkiss Look, can we get on wiv these demands?
Polly (*pencil and notebook at the ready*) Right, I'm ready and waitin'.
Old Min That's the story of your life.
Mrs Purkiss We don't want no more fines.
Maggie What about the wages—we want . . .
Polly Look, will you let me get them down one at a time!

During the above several Dockers enter with their pigeon boxes. They open them up, then try and attract their pets back "home" to the nest

Can we 'ave a bit of 'ush, bruvvers.
Perce Bruvvers?
Tom I fink she's on the turn.
Mrs Purkiss Do you mind, we're 'oldin' a meetin'.
Bert And so are my bloody pigeons up there. Come down, you feathered nits!
Polly Right. Now, anybody want to make a motion?
Perce That's a funny question to ask in the middle of a meetin'.
Winnie Will you belt up! (*She stalks over to Bert*) Them pigeons get more to eat than I do!
Mrs Purkiss Winnie, come and sit down! You're gettin' excited.

Bert Yus, you can't have the baby in the middle of a meetin'.

Winnie returns to her seat beside her mother

Perce What's this meetin' about, Poll?
Polly Bruvver, will you kindly shut up! Right, now what's next?
Maggie We'll go back to work if all stoppages are stopped.
Tom That don't sound right—all stoppages are stopped?
Maggie And premises should be provided where we can eat our grub.
Dot Yus, no more phossy on our bread.
Polly (*proudly*) Right, that's a resolution.
Mrs Purkiss And Kate's got to get her job back.
Polly That's an addendum.
Winnie Or they can get stuffed.
Polly That's an amendment. Now it says 'ere: (*She reads from the book*) "If an amendment to a motion is carried by a majority, it becomes a resolution or a substantive motion, which may subsequently be amended, or complimented by an addendum, if carried by a majority, becomes an original motion." Any questions?
Mrs Purkiss What a load of cobblers. Polly, for Gawd's sake throw that book away and let's put these demands down in our own way.
Perce I reckon you're wastin' yer time, anyway.
Polly Oooh you—fancier of pigeons, you. (*She throws the book at Perce*)
Maggie Polly, are you in charge of this meetin' or ain't yer!
Beattie I wish Kate was 'ere.
Mrs Purkiss Well, she ain't. Now, let's get on wiv it.

During the above, Old Min picks up the book. She now gets up, walks away from the Girls, reading

Old Min "If an amendment to a motion is carried by a majority, it becomes a resolution or a substantive motion."

The Dockers join Old Min

Dockers If an amendment to a motion is carried by a majority—
Old Min It becomes a resolution or a substantive motion.
It becomes an original motion.
Now, what the 'ell's an original motion?

MUSIC: AMENDMENT TO A MOTION

Old Min ⎫ If an amendment to   ⎧ (*singing*
Dockers ⎭ A motion is carried by a majority,   ⎩ *together*)
It becomes a resolution or
A substantive motion.
Old Min It becomes an original motion.
What the 'ell's an original motion?
Oh, I ain't got a perishing notion—
But it becomes an original motion!
Girls If an amendment to a motion

Is carried by a majority,
It becomes a resolution
Or a substantive motion.

All   It becomes an original motion.
What the 'ell's an original motion?
Oh, I ain't got a perishing notion!
But it becomes an original motion—

The Dockers exit

The dancing and singing continues

Jessie and Nell, followed by the rest of the Girls, enter dragging a young Scots Girl. She is poorly dressed, around her shoulders is draped a tattered plaid shawl

Jessie Hey, look, everybody, look what we found.

The Girls crowd around

Mrs Purkiss Who's she?

Polly Where'd yer find her?

Jessie This is one of them Glasgow whores that come down and took our jobs.

Nell One of them what done up Maggie and Dot.

Scots Girl It wasn't me, I tell ye, I've only just arrived.

Winnie Oh, so there's more of yer to come down, eh?

Scots Girl Aye, there were about twenty of us come down yesterday.

Old Min I thought we was supposed to be winning this strike.

Jessie (*grabbing the Scots Girl*) Dot, d'yer recognize her—was she one of them what done yer?

Dot I don't know—I can't remember—let 'er go.

Jessie Let her go, after what they did to you?

Mrs Purkiss What do we do to 'er—take it in turns.

Jessie Tit for tat, that's what I say.

Some of the Girls agree with Jessie

Polly They gotta be taught a lesson.

Mrs Purkiss Do you think by us doin' 'er, the guvnors will stop bringin them down?

Jessie If we show 'em what happens to 'em when they do come down— they might not want to.

The Girls are now divided into two camps. They argue and push among themselves. The Scots Girl, seeing her opportunity, makes to escape but Jessie grabs her

Oh no, you don't.

Jessie throws the Scots Girl to the ground. The Scots Girl sobs in fear

Scots Girl Please, don't touch me—don't touch me—I didna have anything to do with it.

Jessie's "camp" crowd around the Scots Girl

Jessie No, wait—wait a minute. We wanna keep this fair, don't we—above board, like.

Winnie Why? It was eight to one when they done Dot!

Jessie We do things different down 'ere. Like Mrs Purkiss says—we'll take it in turns.

The Girls laugh and argue who shall be next after Jessie

(*prodding the Scots Girl with her boot*) All right, now come on, get up. On yer feet, yer squealin' cow!

Jessie drags the Scots Girl to her feet with the assistance of some of the Girls

(*Shouting*) Come on, will yer. Fight—try and do to me what you did to my two mates.

Jessie's followers taunt the Scots Girl, the others stand helpless. The Scots Girl screams with terror.

Suddenly, as if from nowhere, Kate is in between the Scots Girl and Jessie

Kate Leave 'er alone.

Jessie 'Oo you givin' orders to? Get out of my way.

Kate You wanna fight 'er, you fight me first.

Jessie So that's it. Well, why pick on me—there was plenty of others 'ere was goin' to fight 'er.

Kate I'll fight you.

Mrs Purkiss What good will it do, Kate?

Jessie I'll tell yer. She ain't fightin' me because of this strike, she's fightin' me 'cause she thought I might take Joe away from 'er—that it's me 'e might take to America.

Polly (*going to Kate*) Kate, don't be a fool, go wiv Joe . . .

Kate pushes Polly aside

Kate Now, you wanna fight 'er, you fight me first.

The Scots Girl sees her chance in the midst of this tense situation and runs off

Jessie's supporters would go after her, but their way is barred by Maggie, Mrs Purkiss, Polly, Winnie and Old Min. Kate and Jessie stand facing each other. Then Jessie slings off her shawl and the two Girls circle around each other. Jessie pushes Kate, then jumps back quickly. There are noises and shouts from various Girls. Music adds to the excitement. Suddenly, Kate springs at Jessie. They roll on to the floor amidst screams and yells from the Girls. Polly runs and tries to pull Kate away. Dot then attacks Polly. Winnie suddenly holds her stomach and sinks to the floor

Winnie Ohh, Mum . . .

Mrs Purkiss rushes to Winnie

Mrs Purkiss Winnie!

As the Girls become aware of Winnie's plight, they stop fighting

Winnie Ooh, Mum . . .

Mrs Purkiss Blimey, Win, you don't arf pick your time, don't yer! Come on, 'elp me get her upstairs.

Kate helps Mrs Purkiss with Winnie, and they exit. Louie follows

The Girls take this turn of events quite casually; after all, babies are born anywhere and everywhere in Hope Court

Old Min Well, that's one way of stoppin' a fight.

Polly There must be easier ways.

Beattie I wonder what it'll be, a boy or a girl.

Jessie What's the difference?

Polly Didn't your mum tell you nothin'?

Jessie I mean, it's just another mouth to feed.

Nell I'm only going to 'ave a small family when I get married.

Maggie You mean if you get married.

Nell Don't worry, Mister Right is waiting for me somewhere.

Polly I think he keeps avoidin' yer.

Beattie I wonder what it feels like—when you got a baby inside yer.

Old Min I 'ad twelve. (*After a pause*) 'Appiest days of my life.

Jessie 'Avin' twelve kids?

Old Min When my old man snuffed it.

Nell You got no romance. It must be nice 'avin' yer own baby. One fing that's really yours. 'Oldin' it close—singin' it to sleep.

The Girls are lost in the reverie of Motherhood

Louie enters, she is crying

Jessie What is it? Boy or girl?

Beattie What's 'appened?

Polly What yer cryin' for?

Nell What's the matter?

Louie It was dead.

The Girls are silent

Jessie That's it! That's enough for me! I'm goin' back to work tomorrow!

Kate enters

Polly You can't go back—not now.

Jessie I've 'ad enough, I tell yer.

Nell So 'ave I.

Beattie And me.

Kate 'Oo's talkin' about goin' back? After all we've been through—you wanna give up now?

Jessie It's because of what we been through.

Dot Nothin's goin' to get any better.

Kate (*rushing to them*) But you can't.

Nell You can only take so much.

Jessie And we took enough.

Old Min I told yer—you'll never beat 'em.

Kate But we're not beat.

Jessie We'll see then—we'll go round and see what the others say. We'll take a vote.

The Girls start to move off

Mrs Purkiss appears

Mrs Purkiss (*through her tears*) Listen to me, all of yer—stand still and listen.

The Girls turn

Do you fink what's 'appened to my Winnie 'appened because of this strike? What's just 'appened was one of the reasons why we walked out —we'd 'ad enough—didn't we—we 'ad enough. Now, all of a sudden, you get frightened—you wanna give up. Well, I tell yer if you do you'll deserve everything you get—and you'll get the lot—and gawd 'elp yer.

Annie enters, very excited

Annie Girls—girls it's happened, it's happened. The Directors have agreed to a meeting . . . (*She stops as she surveys the scene of despondency*) What's the matter? What's happened here?

Mrs Purkiss Nuffin' dear lady. Nuffin' at all. What's all this about the Directors?

Annie They've asked for a meeting on Friday.

Kate (*quickly*) Friday?

Annie Myself, the London Trades Council and a member of your Strike Committee. I would like you to be the one Kate.

Kate I don't know.

Maggie You go, Kate . . .

Dot You know 'ow to say the words.

Beattie You can tell 'em . . .

Annie It should be you, Kate . . .

Kate I said I don't know didn't I?

Kate rushes out

Annie What's wrong with her?

Polly What's wrong with all of us. Men!

Louie 'Ave we won, Mrs Besant—is the strike over?

Annie We live in hope. We must wait and see.

The Lighting fades to shadows

SCENE 6

The Waiting Song

The Girls and Dockers dance and/or sing. Several bewhiskered, frock-coated Directors cross through, followed by Annie and Kate

MUSIC: THE WAITING SONG

Girls (*whispering*)   Waiting, waiting,
Always bleedin' waiting,
Waiting, waiting,
Ain't it aggravating!
Waiting, waiting,

> Always bleedin' waiting,
> Waiting, waiting,
> Ain't it aggravating!
>
> Waiting, waiting,
> Always bleedin' waiting.

See score for Syncopated dialogue

(*Singing*) Waiting, waiting,
Everybody's waiting,
You spend your life in waiting
And let the world go by.

Waiting, waiting,
All the world is waiting,
You spend your life in waiting
Till the day you die.

Day you die
Day you die
Day you die
Day you die
Day you die
Day you die
Day you die

All Waiting, waiting,
Always bleedin' waiting,
You spend your life in waiting
And let the day go by.

Waiting, waiting,
Ain't it aggravating,
You spend your life in waiting,
Till the day you die.

Girls You spend nine months in waiting
To see the light of day
And then you 'ave another wait
Until you earns yer pay!

You get a situation
You're waiting, for a rise
But you ain't got an 'ope
Until someone falls down and dies.

Waiting, waiting,	**Men**	Waiting
Everybody's waiting,		Waiting
You spend your life in waiting		Everybody's waiting
And let the day go by.		And let the day go by.

Waiting, waiting,	Waiting
Ain't it aggravating,	Waiting
You spend your life in waiting	Ain't it aggravating
Till the day you die.	Till the day you die.

All

Waiting, waiting,
Always bleedin' waiting,
You spend your life in waiting
And let the day go by.

Waiting, waiting,
Ain't it aggravating,
You spend your life in waiting
Till the day you die.

Waiting, waiting,
Waiting, waiting,
Waiting, waiting.

Waiting, waiting,
Always bleedin' waiting,
You spend your life in waiting
And let the day go by.

Waiting, waiting,
Always bleedin' waiting,
You spend your life in waiting
Till you day you die.

Waiting, waiting,
Waiting, waiting (*etc.*)

Girls (*whispering*)

Waiting, waiting,
Always bleedin' waiting,
Waiting, waiting,
Ain't it aggravating,
Waiting, waiting, waiting.

The song finishes to a whisper as the Lights fade to darkness. In the darkness Annie's voice is heard

Annie GIRLS, WE HAVE WON!

There is a tremendous cheer from the Girls, then silence

SCENE 7
Down by the Docks

In the silence a ship's siren is heard. A street lamp fades up. Under it Kate is standing. The music of "Comes a Time" is heard softly playing. Annie enters; she regards Kate

Annie Kate. (*after a pause*) Kate. The girls are asking where you are. They want you to celebrate the victory with them—they're lost without you. (*She pauses*) We won the battle Kate, but the war's not over—there's much to be done. (*She pauses*) The future, Kate.

Kate (*sadly*) I'm coming. (*She turns to join Annie*)

Joe enters

Kate stares at him unbelievingly, neither of them move

Joe—Joe—it's you—you didn't go! You didn't go! Why, Joe? Tell me why—just say it—the words—tell me why, Joe.

Joe I couldn't find anybody to feed me pigeons!

Kate rushes into Joe's arms: they kiss and walk off

Annie watches them go

SCENE 8

Finale

The Lights come up, as the Girls and Dockers join Annie to sing

MUSIC: THIS LIFE OF MINE (reprise)

Girls Ever since the day that we was born
There's always been someone telling us
What to do and this and that and when
With our three-score years and ten.

Men From now on there'll be some changes made
Things may start going right for us
There'll be no-one pushing us around
We've got our feet on the ground

Company This is our life
Only we can live it
And from now on we're gonna say
What we're gonna do with it

With this life of mine
Maybe I'll change a thing or two
Have a fling or two
I know where I am going to
With this life of mine
Want to have my say
Maybe I'll have to yell and shout
I'll be in, not out
I'll show 'em what it's all about
With this life of mine

Girls I want to clear the air
See just where I'm going
Life is for living and
From now my cup's gonna be overflownig

Company With this life of mine
I'll try and find the truth somehow
Not tomorrow, now
When I take my bow
With this life of mine
With this life of mine.

Joe and Kate enter and take their places with the Company

Joe ⎫	We want to clear the air	⎰	*(singing*
Kate ⎭	See just where we're going	⎱	*together)*
	Life is for living and		
	From now on my cups gonna be overflowing		
Company	With this life of mine		
	I'll try and find the truth somehow		
	Not tomorrow, now		
	When I take my bow		
	With this life of mine		
	With this life of mine!		

CURTAIN

FURNITURE AND PROPERTY LIST

For a general comment see Author's Note, page vi

ACT I

SCENE 1

On stage: 2 or 3 work benches. *On them:* quantity of matchboxes, balsa wood strips, match cutters, match trays

Off stage: Large sack **(Man)**
Empty tray **(Louie)**
Bowler hat **(Nell)**

Personal: **Match Girls:** two pence, sandwiches wrapped in cloth
Jessie: piece of cheese
Min: pig's trotter in newspaper
Potter: religious tract
Mynel: notebook, whistle

SCENE 2

On stage: Line of washing
Street lamp
Crate

Off stage: Banner **(Potter)**
Rope for skipping **(Louie)**

Personal: **Potter:** pamphlets
Annie: shoulderbag with notebook, pencil, copy of *The Link*

SCENE 3

On stage: Grass mat
Pigeon box

Personal: **Kate:** bandage

SCENE 4

On stage: Bunting, replacing clothes line
2 tables with cloths. *On them:* beer barrels and tankards, general wedding food and decorations

Off stage: Copy of *The Link* (**Dot**)

Personal: **Mrs Purkiss:** large handkerchief

SCENE 5

On stage: Street lamp
Crate (for **Kate**)
Small table (for **Annie**)

Personal: **Kate:** pen, paper, writing board

SCENE 6

On stage: Small table (from Scene 5)
Small table. *On it:* account books, pamphlets, pen, books
Chair
Hatstand

Off stage: Telegram (**Annie**)

Personal: **Shaw:** copy of *The Link*

ACT II

SCENE 1

On stage: Line of washing as Scene 2
Crate
Bench

Off stage: Ball (**Louie**)
2 suitcases, pots, pans, oddments (**Polly**)
2 suitcases, oddments (**Beattie, Nell**)
Hand-cart (**Joe**)
Suitcase (**Louie**)
Cup of water (**Winnie**)

SCENE 2

On stage: Decorative screen
Table. *On it:* cloth, tray, teapot, milk jug, sugar bowl, 3 cups, 3
saucers, 3 teaspoons, plate of sandwiches, 3 table napkins
2 chairs. *On them:* 2 newspapers

SCENE 3

On stage: Platform or wooden box
7 placards (for **Girls** and **Dockers**)

SCENE 4

On stage: Street lamp

SCENE 5

On stage: Line of washing as Scene 1
Various boxes and stools
Board reading COMMITEA MEETING—BELT UP (for **Old Min**)

Off stage: Pigeon boxes **(Dockers)**

Personal: **Polly:** book, pencil, notebook

SCENE 7

On stage: Street lamp

LIGHTING PLOT

The following plot gives cues indicated in the action
Additional cues, for songs, etc., may be incorporated at the discretion of the
director
Property fittings required: 1 street lamp
Various settings on open stage

ACT I

To open: General effect of summer sunshine seeping through one
dusty factory window

Cue 1   As Scene 1 closes   (Page 7)
*Cross-fade to dingy, shadowy courtyard lighting, street lamp
lit*

Cue 2   **Dockers** enter   (Page 10)
Brighten general lighting slightly

Cue 3   General exit of **Dockers** and **Girls**   (Page 12)
Fade overall lighting slightly

Cue 4   **Kate:** "I'll tell yer on the way."   (Page 16)
*Brighten overall lighting for **Dockers'** and **Girls'** entrance and
dance*

Cue 5   At end of Scene 2   (Page 17)
*Cross-fade to spot on **Kate** and **Joe***

Cue 6   At end of Scene 3   (Page 19)
*Cross-fade to spots on **Winnie** and **Bert***

Cue 7   **Winnie** and **Bert** (singing) "something about you, my
love."   (Page 20)
Bring up general lighting to full

Cue 8   At end of "Knees Up" routine   (Page 23)
Fade to Black-out

Cue 9   At start of Scene 5   (Page 23)
*Bring up spot on street lamp and **Kate***

Cue 10   **Kate:** ". . . will succeed in your undertaking."   (Page 23)
*Bring up spot on **Annie***

Cue 11   **Kate:** "you have shown us girls".   (Page 23)
*Fade spot on **Kate***

Cue 12   As Scene 6 opens   (Page 24)
Bring up general lighting in bookshop

| *Cue* 13 | At end of Scene 6
Cross-fade to shadowy exterior lighting | **(Page 27)** |
| *Cue* 14 | As song: WE'RE GONNA SHOW 'EM starts
Increase overall lighting to full | **(Page 28)** |

ACT II

To open: Effect of hot, dusty sunshine

Cue 15	At end of Scene 1 *Cross-fade to concentrated lighting on drawing-room area*	**(Page 37)**
Cue 16	**Annie:** "We'll see." *Fade to spot on **Kate** for opening of Scene 3*	**(Page 39)**
Cue 17	At close of Scene 3 *Cross-fade to shadowy exterior effect for Docks, spot covering street lamp*	(Page 40)
Cue 18	**Jessie** and **Joe** (singing, off): "You say, 'I will'." *Fade to Black-out, then up to full on Hope Court, morning light*	**(Page 42)**
Cue 19	**Annie:** "We must wait and see." *Fade lighting to overall shadowy effect for WAITING SONG, Scene 6*	**(Page 48)**
Cue 20	At end of song *Fade to Black-out. After **Girls** cheer, fade up to shadowy Docks lighting, as Cue 17*	**(Page 50)**
Cue 21	After **Kate** and **Joe** exit *Bring up overall lighting to full for Finale*	(Page 51)

EFFECTS PLOT

ACT I

No cues

ACT II

Cue 1	As Scene 4 opens *Ship's siren sounds*	(Page 41)
Cue 2	Jessie: "Neither would I." *Ship's siren*	(Page 41)
Cue 3	As Scene 7 opens *Ship's siren*	(Page 50)

MADE AND PRINTED IN GREAT BRITAIN BY
LATIMER TREND & COMPANY LTD PLYMOUTH

MADE IN ENGLAND